Table

MW01193507

Acknowledgements

This one goes out to my sister, Suzanne Babb, the NYC food activist/urban gardener extraordinaire who inspired this book. You grow, girl! I also dedicate this book to my son and sunshine of my life, Thomas Christopher Neely. May you always bloom where you're planted, my sweet boy. - Carol-Ann Hoyte, editor

I want to thank my many models—tomato, eggplant, sweet potato, grapes, all you other wonderful fruits, vegetables, plants, bees, and cows (oh, and the occasional human)—who patiently posed for this book. I would also like to thank Carol-Ann for challenging me to make food look good in black and white. And, finally, a thank-you to my parents whose love of photography they passed on to me—this is for you. - Norie Wasserman, photographer.

Permissions

"Frog in the Bucket" by April Halprin Wayland, which appeared in *Cricket Magazine* (August 2000), appears here with permission from the author.

"Dance of the Mushrooms" by J. Patrick Lewis, which appeared in Myra Cohn Livingston's *Animal, Vegetable, Mineral: Poems About Small Things* (HarperCollins Publishers, 1994), appears here with permission from the author.

Poetry Forms

Introduction

Dear Tomato: An International Crop of Food and Agriculture Poems is a cornucopia of dietary treats. No hodgepodge here; its delectable offerings take you from farmyard to table. Vegans, vegetarians, omnivores, and carnivores will all find fare to feast on at this banquet.

At a time when eating habits have drastically changed, it's great to have such a candid yet refreshing view of agriculture. We are out of sync when it comes to seasonality, eating summer fruits, like melons and strawberries, in December. 'Snap' used to precede 'peas'; now, as an acronym for the Supplemental Nutrition Assistance Program, it's a way for families in the US to purchase food. Families everywhere are relying more on eating out, rather than preparing home-cooked meals.

Dear Tomato captures the spirit and personal experiences of growing and eating food, delving into childhood memories of growing up on a farm or refusing to eat yucky peas or standing in line at the food bank.

The poems are dripping with international flavor, a reminder that food is universal. We must continue to be aware of where our food comes from, be mindful of the ones who grow and harvest it, give dignity and fare wages to all along the food chain. Justice is not about 'just us' but must include the care of land and animals as well.

There's room enough for all at the table of food and social justice. Applause and appreciation go out to those who contributed to this book; through their experiences and humility, they have captured the essence of the human spirit. What's for dessert is up to you.

Karen Washington
Urban Farmer
Bronx, New York

Editor's Note: Karen Washington was one of the five recipients of the 2014 James Beard Foundation Leadership Award. You grow, girl!

A Farmer's Prayer

Sun sun,

        not too warm.

Rain rain,

        without harm.

Sprouts sprout,

        healthy-tall.

Harvest harvest,

        come the fall;

        fare aplenty,

        food for all.

- ROBERT HEIDBREDER (CANADA)

My grandpa and grandma, who farmed a small farm on the Prairies, wished a prayer wish like this every year.

This is what I like to think of as a double duty poem since the first noun also becomes the first verb in each stanza or vice versa.

The Dream

I wake slowly,
trying to remember my dream.

I stir gently,
not wanting to leave my dream.

Suddenly,
I burst awake!

I lift my head,
throw off the covers,
look up—

Sun!

Warmth above me,
life surging in me,
growing,
breathing,
changing—

GREEN.

This green was my dream—
the long dream
in my
deep
seed
sleep.

- MARY LEE HAHN (UNITED STATES)

As seeds grow in rows,
a lightning strike scares away
multitudes of crows.

- CHARLES WATERS (UNITED STATES)

5 A.M.

I am a girl sitting with her father, sipping hot cocoa,
and chewing peanut butter toast,
then tiptoeing out the door.
It is still dark

as Dad and Joginder,
our farm manager from India,
load long irrigation pipes
onto the wagon hooked to the tractor.

I am a girl waiting,
arranging acorns into patterns on the ground.
When the wagon is full,
Dad, Joginder, and I climb onto the tractor.

At the walnut orchard,
Dad and Joginder place two pipes
on the ground between the first row of trees
and hook them together.

I am the girl
sitting on the tractor seat,
holding the steering wheel.

At Dad's signal,
I am the girl letting her foot off the clutch,
pressing her foot on the gas pedal,
slowly driving the tractor down the row.

Dad and Joginder walk alongside.
Dad says, "Okay."
I am the girl gently, firmly pressing the brake.
They unload two more pipes.

I am driving,
then stopping while they unload,
then driving again.
The sun is rising.

The first time I saw the sun rise,
I thought it was a spaceship landing
on the levee.
But now I am older,

old enough to drive this tractor.
I know it is the sun,
and the sun makes everything
orange with morning.

40 more pipes to go.

- APRIL HALPRIN WAYLAND (UNITED STATES)

Dawn mist swoops upon
the evenly furrowed fields,
soothing the scarred earth.

- J H RICE (ENGLAND)

The Diversity of Dirt

Matching footprints
Dirt, designed
Blessing of earth
Dirt, divined
Drilling on land
Dirt, maligned
Processing clay
Dirt, refined
Mountain journey
Dirt, inclined
Muddy water
Dirt, entwined
Filthy substance
Dirt, defined.

- CHARLES WATERS (UNITED STATES)

Root Veggies

I despise that shameful swagga
of an unclothed rutabaga,

and yellow yams are very rude,
especially when in the nude.

Those prancing parsnips never clothed,
that's one sight I've always loathed.

I'd like to coldly cast a curse
on unbecoming beets and, worse,

those turnips lacking underwear;
it pains me so, but I just stare.

Lastly, lowly burdock roots
are clad in nothing and in cahoots.

It's all wrong and so distressing.
I prefer them in some dressing.

- KEN SLESARIK (UNITED STATES)

Compost Bin

Hungry
for husks,
pips, and peels—
a splendiferous feast of
leftovers.

- MICHELLE HEIDENRICH BARNES (UNITED STATES)

A Potato's Valentine

The cream of the crop
The tuber to beat
You're so delicious
A vegetable treat

Your skin is a-peeling
My knees turn to mash
whenever I see you
A spud that is smash

In your smart jacket
a treat for my eye
You are multi-talented
Boil, bake, or fry

Let's grow old together
Have an offshoot or two
Have fun in the earth
while we're still new

I'll just cut the waffle
Please be my friend
Let's put down roots
Together to the end

- PHILIPPA RAE (ENGLAND)

cut the waffle: keep to the point

Grandpa's Garden

We forked my grandpa's garden and pulled out pesky weeds,
dug in buckets of compost, then planted rows of seeds.

The sparrows pecked the seedlings so we zigzagged them
    with twine.
The slugs chomped at the cabbage. We dropped offenders
    into brine.

Young rabbits ate the lettuce till we fenced the garden in.
Then blackbirds pecked the raspberries. It seemed we couldn't
    win.

But Grandpa strung the bushes with big nets to keep birds out.
We tied things that clanged and clattered when the breeze
    blew them about.

And after lots of watering, more weeding, and some sun,
we began to pick our produce, and this was much more fun.

We podded such sweet tender peas, scrubbed crunchy carrots
    clean,
had lots of greens for salads, and picked two kinds of bean.

The food we grew at Grandpa's all tasted really great.
What's more, I've grown three inches—thanks to everything I ate.

- FRANCES HERN (CANADA)

Helping Grandma

In the garden, on my knees,
grateful for the cooling breeze,
I am weeding Grandma's peas.
And I don't even like them.

Sister weeds her corn with ease.
She won't help, ignores my pleas,
leaves me here alone with peas.
And I don't even like them.

Mom says that it's good for me
to be helping family,
so I weed peas eternally.
And I don't even like them.

- CINDY BREEDLOVE (UNITED STATES)

Peas

I will not eat those yucky peas,
not even if you say, "Oh, please",
not even if you scream and shout,
not even if you dance about.

I will not eat them even if
I have to sit with legs gone stiff.
I will not eat them hot or cold.
I will not eat them when I'm old.

I will not put a single one
inside my mouth or in my tum.
And if you tell me there's no pud,
I'll fold my arms and bellow, "Good!"

So let's see who will win this war.
I've won the ones that came before.
I'll win this too—just wait and see—
for I will NEVER eat a pea!

- CONRAD BURDEKIN (ENGLAND)

Vegan

Serve me veggies; serve me fruits:
bulbs, tubers, buds, roots,
flowers, seeds, stems, leaves.
Never these, I beg you, please:
meat, fish, milk, eggs,
chicken wings, turkey legs,
anything with eyes or feet.
These I simply will not eat!

- STEPHANIE SALKIN (UNITED STATES)

Soya beans lay pressed,
yielding milk, while cows can laugh
safely from the hills.

- KIMBERLY O'BRIEN (ENGLAND)

My Brother, the Vegetarian

When my brother visits our house,
we simmer eggplant in tomato sauce,
boil a pot of rice and beans,
and bake his favorite lemon cake.
He brings his children
and gives us each a book.
Sometimes he plays basketball
before dinner.
He always asks, "What's new?"

When we sit down to eat,
we don't ask
why he won't eat ham
or if he'll eat turkey on Thanksgiving (he won't)
or what's the matter with meat.
We clink our water glasses,
pass the bread,
laugh—
and leave room for cake.

- ANN MALASPINA (UNITED STATES)

Gone Shopping

Basket in tow,
I go to the garden,
reach for Eggplant,
ripe and regal
in her purple splendor,
sunlight bouncing off
her satin skin.
"She is too beautiful
for roasting,"
my eyes tell me.
I almost agree,
but then,
my stomach growls.

- NIKKI GRIMES (UNITED STATES)

Fair Is Fair

(a lesson in Fair Trade)

Mother's coffee,
Father's tea,
Sister's cocoa—
all might be
a farmer's only
chance to give
his family
a chance to live.

- MATT FORREST ESENWINE (UNITED STATES)

Food Bank Withdrawal

My hand sweats
in Mom's grasp.
My tummy rumbles;
my head aches.
No breakfast this morning;
no dinner last night.

I shift and shuffle—
left foot,
right,
left again.
"Stand still," Mom whispers.

This line is taking
forever.
When will it be
our turn?

Cart after cart
filled with rice, beans,
bread, peanut butter,
canned fruit, cereal
rolls out of the darkened
warehouse.
Moms, kids, old people
shuffle forward
to claim
their bounty.

Finally,
it is our turn.
I grab the next cart
and roll it straight
to the parking lot.
Mom has to steer
around the cars.

I'm so happy
we have food.
Maybe it will last
until Dad hears
back from the factory.

- BRIDGET MAGEE (UNITED STATES)

Grapes of Laughter

Here's to you
Dolores Huerta
And you Cesar Chavez
I clink my plate
against your plate
A toast with jam
made out of grapes
that taste just great

A toast to you
And then some sips
of grape juice
make me lick my lips
'Cause the finest juice
is the grape juice made
from grapes picked
by pickers paid
a fair wage

When you treat
workers like you should
it just makes grapes
taste good

And when the grapes are good
the jam is good
And when the jam is good
O man it's good

So here's to pickers
And picketers too
A toast with jelly
Good health to you

Mmmm justice
just is so tasty
Justice
just makes
juice and jam
jelly and wine
taste so fine

- ROBERT PRIEST (CANADA)

Ron Finley, Activist Gardener

Ron Finley broke the law.
He planted squash on a strip of dirt by the curb in front of his
    house.
He wanted to turn a food desert into an edible forest.
He wanted to turn a health problem into a community
    solution.
He wanted to turn vacant land into a painted canvas.

When people heard Ron got a ticket for gardening,
they started a petition nine hundred people signed.

Ron Finley changed the law.
All over LA, it's now okay to plant food between the sidewalk
    and the street.
Neighbors meet to dig, plant, weed, and harvest.
Kids get shovels and something to do and all the fresh
    tomatoes they can eat.
Ron Finley planted squash but look what he grew.

- ELIZABETH STEINGLASS (UNITED STATES)

Iroquois Garden

Three sisters
dwell together
in a garden.

The eldest
stands statue tall,
proud and straight,
silky hair aflutter,
pale green shawl
wrapped tightly
round her ear.

The second sister,
prickly as a porcupine,
meanders one way and
another,
blanketing her sisters' feet,
hiding golden
treasures.

The youngest sister
springs from earth—
circling, winding,
whirling, twirling—
a dancer reaching
new heights,
binding sisters
all together.

Three sisters:
Corn,
Squash,
and Bean.

- **BUFFY SILVERMAN (UNITED STATES)**

Hundreds of years before Europeans settled North America, the Iroquois grew corn, squash, and beans in their gardens. Corn plants grew tall and straight, providing support for beans. Squash plants grew thick and prickly, shading the earth and keeping it moist. Weeds could not sprout under thick squash leaves, and the plants' irritating spines deterred raccoons, deer, and other animals. Bean plants took nitrogen from the air and fixed it with their roots, enriching the soil. Many people still grow the Three Sisters together in gardens.

Oats, wheat, raisins, corn.
Fields of toil dance in one bowl,
with a splash of milk.

- KIMBERLY O'BRIEN (ENGLAND)

I Sing the Fruit Exotic

Speak to me
of hairy hedgehogs
five-pointed stars
and stinky spiny things,
of dragon eyes
outer space creatures
and dinosaur-egg-looking things.

I'll sing to you
of ram-bu-tan
ca-ram-bo-la
and du-ri-an,
of lon-gan
ki-wa-no
and cher-i-moy-a.

Speak to me
of surprising
unusual
fruit
and
"exotic-ilicious!"

I will sing.

- CORY CORRADO (CANADA)

Dance of the Mushrooms

Mushrooms tipping their caps—
this is all you ever see.

But when night falls
from the clouds,
and no one is watching,
they brown shyly
and begin to dance.

Bowing softly,
they waltz in the dark
to the wind hymning
through the trees.
But when light falls
from the clouds,

mushrooms tipping their caps—
this is all you ever see.

- J. PATRICK LEWIS (UNITED STATES)

What I Know about Figs

I know about rows of fig trees
on scorching hot summer days.
I know about drawing aside the curtain
of their great green leaves
and reaching into their cool darkness
for those plump black balloons.

I know about placing each fig
gingerly in my bucket
until it's full.

I know about holding the bucket
and climbing the ladder,
rung by rung,
that leans against our shed.

I know about gently placing figs
on raised rows of the aluminum roof,
covering them with netting,
climbing down
to fill my bucket
again
and again
and again.

I know about climbing up
days later to see
that they're not ready.

I know about waiting,
long hot days
of waiting.

I know about climbing up the ladder
to finally peel them off the hot aluminum.

I know about
hot summer nights on the farm,
vanilla ice cream
topped with dried figs
like chewy caramels.

- APRIL HALPRIN WAYLAND (UNITED STATES)

Pumpkin

Planted seeds.
Ground was dry.
Watered well
and wished for pie.
Thanksgiving came;
I cleaned my plate!

Gourd things come
to those who wait.

- **MATT FORREST ESENWINE (UNITED STATES)**

A Ripe Peach

Fragrant flesh gives
beneath gentle pressure upon downy softness.
A bite brings juice so flavourful
trickling down throat, chin.
Breathe in the sweetness of summer
stored in its rosy blush.

- FRANCES HERN (CANADA)

Baby Veg

I like baby sweetcorn
because it's tasty.
I like baby carrots
because they're sweet.
Baby vegetables taste *much* nicer
and are *much* more interesting
than grown-up vegetables.

I used to think that sprouts
were baby cabbages.
But they're not baby cabbages at all.
They are only *pretending* to be
baby cabbages.
Really, they are grown-up vegetables
in disguise—
which explains their grown-up taste.
Yuck!

- J H RICE (ENGLAND)

Crops

Cabbages, lined up in
Rows
Of hundreds,
Prepare for graduation after
Starting out as seeds.

- CHARLES WATERS (UNITED STATES)

Farmers Markets

Farmers' fresh produce from local suppliers
Asparagus trucked in for bag-bringing buyers
Ripe scarlet strawberries, stems green as May
Mauve and pink peonies pouf a bouquet
Early birds snag plumpest blueberries first
Rollicking fiddlers tap feet, croon their verse
Summer's abloom with sweet cherries and corn

Melons and mint scent the hot July morn
August arrives bringing cosmos and poppy
Raspberries, jam berries, juicy and sloppy
Kale in the summer, kale in the fall
Eggs, by the dozen, at each farmer's stall
Tomatoes in red, yellow, orange, and brown
Seasonal treats farmed for markets in town

- HELEN KEMP ZAX (UNITED STATES)

Who's the Unclucky One?

I've a clip on my leg, and one on my wing.
I'm a bird, but I don't sing.

I'm barred from the yard, shut in a cage.
I work all day for no wage.

For meals, I peck at a pile of muck.
No wonder my voice is a grumbly cluck!

But I've treats for your tea
Guess them - and guess me.
You'll find them in shells, in sixes or twelves,
stacked up in boxes on grocery shelves.

Guessed? So what could I be?

- KATE WILLIAMS (WALES)

Answer: A battery hen

A Famous Egg

A famous egg
fell off a wall,
and now we know his tale.
But what about the crazy chef
who placed him in a pail?
Why, he fried him up and served him
with a tasty side of kale!

- CATHERINE RONDINA (CANADA)

A Tale of Two Hens

All day and every night, trapped in a cage.
My world is the size of an A4 page.
Can't flap my wings or stretch my legs.
Like a machine, I just keep laying eggs.
Cold hard wire, no cosy nest.
My feathers fall out, I am so stressed.
Will I ever feel the sun or see the sky?
Must I be in this prison till the day I die?

I get up early and bask in the sun,
flap my wings, jump and run.
I scratch in the dirt with my feet,
searching for juicy worms to eat.
My friends and I all cluck and play,
then find a nice warm nest and lay.
It feels so wonderful to be free.
Oh, I'm as happy as a hen can be!

So when next you're out for brunch
or ordering an omelette for your lunch,
at the supermarket or wherever you shop,
before you buy your eggs, please STOP!
And think ...

- CAROL SCHOLZ (AUSTRALIA)

Free-Range

Chickens lay hale and hearty eggs
when they get to stretch their legs.

- ALAN MURPHY (IRELAND)

Gardener's Math Poems

20 mph breeze
<u>x1 dandelion gone to seed</u>
20 hours of pulling weeds

      <u>rows</u>
hoe) soil

      <u>living quilt</u>
rows) garden

(basil – leaves) + (tomato / 5) + oilvinegarmozzarella =
      caprese salad

     rain
   <u>x sun</u>
 sprouting
  growing
<u>+flowering</u>
harvest time

1 strawberry plant + 3 ripe red berries / rabbit + bird + me =
    1 sweet nibble, remainder 0

- MARY LEE HAHN (UNITED STATES)

The Emperor's Greenhouse

Munchily crunchily
Roman Tiberius:
Emperor, conqueror,
Cucumber hound.

Summer or wintertime,
Gherkin-delirious,
Mirrorstone* let him en-
Joy them year round.

- MICHELLE HEIDENRICH BARNES (UNITED STATES)

*Ancient Roman gardeners used structures similar to our modern greenhouses to make sure that Emperor Tiberius had cucumbers on his table every day of the year. According to Pliny the Elder, they were grown under frames glazed with mirrorstone, which we now know as Selenite—a transparent, crystalline rock.

Small, smaller, smallest

So Alice said she was going to do
square yard vegetable growing.
She could be self-sufficient
through the four seasons.
Rinda turned red and said
she could better it
with her square foot
vegetable garden,
which would feed her
and her son
for the year.
At which point,
Chip chipped in
with his now-legendary
square inch vegetable garden,
which—for 365 days—
could feed
a disinterested slug
on a diet.

- ROB WALTON (ENGLAND)

Catalogue of Woes

These are ways
to harm a farm:
a flooding storm,
a locust swarm,
a wilting blight,
a weevil's bite,
a killing frost,
a car's exhaust,
a scorching blaze,
a smoky haze,
a year of drought
day in, day out,
a loan foreclosed,
a barn bulldozed.

In spite of all
that might befall
a fragile crop,
nothing can stop,
nothing can still,
a farmer's will.

- STEVEN WITHROW (UNITED STATES)

Hoe Observing the Farmer

He knows a hoe.
Never letting go.
Holds me steady in his grip,
lifts me up to rip against the weight of air.
Then he pulls me back, bearing down,
yielding to the power of the ground.
Holds me steady in his grip,
never letting go.
He knows
a hoe.

- APRIL HALPRIN WAYLAND (UNITED STATES)

The Plight of the Honeybee

The collapse of the bee population
is a buzz that's been heard round the nation.
Though safe from disease,
crops are killing the bees
with pesticide-laced pollination.

- **MICHELLE HEIDENRICH BARNES (UNITED STATES)**

Wreaths of flower heads,
pollen-laced with pesticides,
mourn a lack of bees.

- KIMBERLY O'BRIEN (ENGLAND)

Growing Greens

Mommy grows flowers.
She thins them and feeds them.
She prunes them and pots them
and waters and weeds them.

Daddy grows grass.

Mommy grows ivy
and bushes and hedges
that grow by the garden
and over the ledges.

Daddy grows grass.

Mommy grows roses
of all shapes and sizes.
She takes them to fairs
and often wins prizes.

Daddy grows grass.

Well, actually...
sometimes Daddy grows flowers—
pretty yellow dandelions that cover the lawn.
But Daddy pulls them up

to grow more grass.

- MATT FORREST ESENWINE (UNITED STATES)

In My Garden

Last summer, after the magnolias failed to bloom,
well after the tulips lost their heads,
after the rains ceased,
most of the grass died in my garden.

Nothing much to be done
with that sorry checkerboard!

Then with shorter August days,
one small pansy settled in a rough, dry patch.
The white flower, blushing violet,
took comfort in my garden.

Too soon autumn leaves covered it.
Later snow, ice, cold rain, and snow again.

When April's sun melted all that,
well before the magnolias, the tulips,
before the juncos in their pinafores,
that pansy defied the scraggly lawn,
bloomed again in my garden.

Then this morning—not too early, not too late—
I startled at a rabbit:
A big brown rabbit, with sharp-tipped ears,
black eyes the size of wild chokecherries,
and a cartoon-perfect cotton ball tail.
In my garden,
in
my
garden!

It ambled forward,
stopped at the pansy,
nibbled the purple petals,
and hopped away,
leaving just enough
to grow another blossom
in my garden.

- JC SULZENKO (CANADA)

I Would Like to Eat Grass

I would like to eat grass.
It's free and green and looks healthy,
and horses and cows and sheep and small wriggly creatures
all eat grass.

But if I *could* eat grass, I might be bored and sometimes,
for a treat,
I would eat a nettle, a thistle, or a dandelion.
And maybe I'd think about how nice they taste,
but then someone, somewhere, would tell me
(because someone, somewhere, will always tell you such
things)
that too many weeds are bad for you.
"Dandelions are bad for your teeth," they'd say.
"And thistles make you fat."

You might never get it right
when it comes to food,
even if you could eat grass.

- J H RICE (ENGLAND)

Food for Thought

There's junk food and fresh food
Give your tongue a fright food
Cold food and hot food
Can't eat another bite food
Plain food and novel food
Lick your lips and grovel food
Food that's packed with nutrients
And food that's just a joke
Food that makes us fit as frogs
And food that makes us croak.

- GREG O'CONNELL (NEW ZEALAND)

Frog in a Bucket

We bought a frog
at the farmers market.
We bought a frog,
and we bought him a bucket.

We were going away for a week to the lake,
and whenever we stopped,
I was scared Frog would bake
in the truck when we stopped for a drink, so I brought him,
and he swished back and forth
in the bucket we bought him.

We bought a frog
at the farmers market.
We bought a frog,
and we bought him a bucket.

Have you ever been shopping
inside a big store
by the crackers and catsup and
tried to ignore
a young kid (that kid's me) walking past with a bucket—
and if you look in, there's a frog looking up it?

We bought a frog
at the farmers market.
We bought a frog,
and we bought him a bucket.

If a boy brought his horse there, he'd tie it outside.
If a girl snuck a cat in, she'd stuff it inside
of her sweater (nervous and hoping that no one would get
her).
But I take my bucket wherever I get
'cause a frog in a bucket's a portable pet.
I take him to movies. I roll him on skates.

So buy one—a frog in a bucket is great!

- APRIL HALPRIN WAYLAND (UNITED STATES)

I really did *buy a frog at a farmers market!*

Contain Your Imagination

Raspberries trellis up old wicker chairs.
Parsley in teakettles sits on the stairs.

Blackberries thrive in Dad's busted-up dinghy.
Pole beans in wash baskets grow tall and stringy.

Cabbages nestle in cracked kiddie pools.
Peppers in wheelbarrows glisten like jewels.

Summer squash tumbles from Mom's torn rain boots.
Tomatoes in toolboxes show off their fruits.

Cucumbers spill out from watering cans.
Seedlings sprout quickly in used muffin pans.

Strawberries thrive in a little red wagon.
Basil erupts from a porcelain flagon.

Colander, egg carton, bathtub, or wok?
Containers with whimsy make gardening rock!

- B.J. LEE (UNITED STATES)

The Peace Rose

I flower for hope,

calm pinks and creams,

spreading out my tranquil dreams.

I grow for trust

in love's increase.

I am the fragrant rose called...

Peace.

- ROBERT HEIDBREDER (CANADA)

My grandmother loved roses—climbing, cascading, upright, and wild. Her favourite was the Peace rose. The story she often told was that it first came to North America in April 1945, on the very day Berlin fell, and a truce was declared. The Nazi threat was over. She said she planted it among her vegetables since it always reminded her of the great peace working in a garden brings.

Let's Grow!

It's springtime in the city.
Things are sprouting down below.
But our building isn't blooming,
so let's get to work. Let's grow!

First on the bill: each windowsill
that's sunny, not too hot.
A tulip here, a crocus there—
pass me another pot!

Now, hm, let's see: this balcony
that used to seem so small.
Flowers, herbs, tomatoes—
yes, there's room to grow them all.

One last stop: the large rooftop
has lots of empty space.
We build big wooden boxes
and plant veggies every place.

Before you even know it,
we'll have lettuce for our lunch
and, with a little TLC,
fresh carrots by the bunch.

We're tired and we're dirty
and we're happy 'cause we know
that we got our building blooming,
and it's going to grow, grow, GROW!

- TIFFANY STONE (CANADA)

Window Garden

Dear Tomato,
I hope you won't mind
living in the city.
I'll give you my favorite spot
by the window
where the sun shines
every afternoon.
If your leaves droop
or your soil dries,
I'll be your rain.
I'll fill a cup and give
your roots a long, cool drink.
You've got no competition here,
no weeds to steal from you.
When you bloom,
I'll open the window
to let in the bees,
or maybe I can be the breeze
that spreads your pollen.
I'll watch your yellow stars shine
and fade, your small green moons
swell and turn red.
When they are ripe and ready,
I'll pluck them from your tired stem
and pop them into my mouth.
I'll feast and thank you.

Don't worry. I won't eat them all.
I'll save some for their seeds,
so we can grow together
next year too.

- **ELIZABETH STEINGLASS (UNITED STATES)**

The Old Farmer's Song

At the edge of the world, I graze my sheep,
where storm clouds swirl, and the valley cuts deep.

I've farmed this land for fifty years,
calloused my hands on shovels and shears,

raised my cattle as best I could,
a constant battle in thick bog mud.

But a soaring hawk, a hare on the run,
an early walk with the rising sun,

a horse's flanks as they heave and steam,
frost on the banks of a snow-melt stream

make my old heart beat to the rhythm of the farm,
the low pig grunts and the cows in the barn.

Till I'm ash and dust, till I'm dead and gone,
I'll be in these hills, and I'll sing this song.

- MATT GOODFELLOW (ENGLAND)

Made in the USA
Charleston, SC
28 October 2015